# WHAT ARE GRASSLANDS?

LAURA LORIA

## Britannica
### Educational Publishing

IN ASSOCIATION WITH

ROSEN
EDUCATIONAL SERVICES

Published in 2019 by Britannica Educational Publishing (a trademark of Encyclopædia Britannica, Inc.) in association with The Rosen Publishing Group, Inc.
29 East 21st Street, New York, NY 10010

Distributed exclusively by Rosen Publishing.
To see additional Britannica Educational Publishing titles, go to rosenpublishing.com.

First Edition

**Britannica Educational Publishing**
J.E. Luebering: Executive Director, Core Editorial
Mary Rose McCudden: Editor, Britannica Student Encyclopedia

**Rosen Publishing**
Amelie von Zumbusch: Editor
Matt Cauli: Series Designer
Tahara Anderson: Book Layout
Cindy Reiman: Photography Manager
Sherri Jackson: Photo Researcher

**Library of Congress Cataloging-in-Publication Data**

Names: Loria, Laura, author.
Title: What are grasslands? / Laura Loria.
Description: First edition. | New York : Britannica Educational Publishing, in Association with Rosen Educational Services, 2019. | Series: Let's find out! Biomes | Audience: Grades 1–5. | Includes bibliographical references and index.
Identifiers: LCCN 2018010013| ISBN 9781508106968 (library bound) | ISBN 9781508107101 (paperback) | ISBN 9781508107316 (6 pack)
Subjects:  LCSH: Grassland ecology—Juvenile literature.
Classification: LCC QH541.5.P7 L69 2019 | DDC 577.4—dc23
LC record available at https://lccn.loc.gov/2018010013

*Manufactured in the United States of America*

**Photo credits**: Cover and interior pages background 06 Photo/Shuterstock.com; pp. 4, 26 ©Encyclopædia Britannica, Inc.; p. 5 © Brian Kell; pp. 6, 11, 13 Auscape/Universal Images Group/Getty Images; p. 7 Jason Patrick Ross/Shutterstock.com; pp. 8, 12 © Digital Vision/Getty Images; p. 9 © Joss/Fotolia; p. 10 Michael Nichols/National Geographic Magazines/Getty Images; p. 14 Tim Fitzharris/Minden Pictures/Getty Images; p. 15 Jim Brandenburg/Minden Pictures/Getty Images; p. 16 Regula Heeb-Zweifel/AWL Images/Getty Images; p. 17 © Margouillat/Fotolia; p. 18 © Chip and Rosa Maria Peterson; p. 19 © A.M. Wettach/Shostal Associates; p. 20 © Gerald Cubitt-Bruce Coleman Ltd.; p. 21 Moelyn Photos/Moment/Getty Images; p. 22 Sebastien Burel/Fotolia; p. 23 Tom Reichner/Shutterstock.com; p. 24 © PRILL Mediendesign/Fotolia; p. 25 BGSmith/Shutterstock.com; p. 27 Dhoxaxl/Fotolia; p. 28 © Tom Koerner/U.S. Fish and Wildlife Service; p. 29 Robert Postma/Design Pics/First Light/Getty Images.

# CONTENTS

# FIELDS OF GREEN

When you look around the area you live in, what do you see that makes it different from other places on Earth?

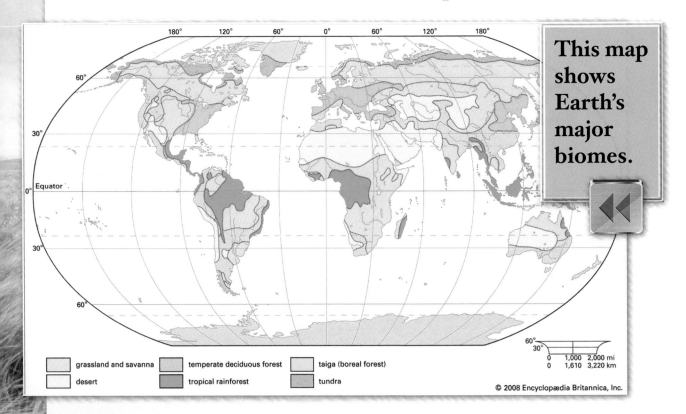

This map shows Earth's major biomes.

| | | |
|---|---|---|
| grassland and savanna | temperate deciduous forest | taiga (boreal forest) |
| desert | tropical rainforest | tundra |

You might notice that you live in an area with lots of hills, or maybe your town is very flat. It might be hot and dry most of the time, or the area might get lots of rain. There might be certain animals that live in your area that aren't found other places. Your hometown has natural features that are **unique**, and it is part of a larger area called a biome.

A biome is a large region of Earth that has a certain climate and certain types of living things. One of the major biomes on Earth is the grasslands. Grasslands are places that get enough rain for grasses to grow but not enough to support forests.

**Oglala National Grassland, seen here, is in northwestern Nebraska.**

# THE FORMATION OF GRASSLANDS

Grasslands once covered about 20 percent of the land on Earth. They stretch between forests and deserts. Grasslands near forests are wetter and have some trees. Those near deserts are drier and have less plant life. The grasslands began to form millions of years ago, when Earth's climate was

The Mitchell Grass Downs in Australia, shown here, hosts a variety of plant life.

**THINK ABOUT IT**

As the climate of Earth changes, how might grasslands be affected?

becoming cooler and drier. Over time, grasslands sprung up in different parts of the world. Some were formed as tropical rainforests began to dry out. Others were formed as the result of cold, dry periods known as ice ages.

Grasslands were also formed by what people would call natural disasters, such as wildfires, floods, and droughts. These events would clear an area of larger plants and change the soil conditions. From these cleared spaces, grasses would grow and take over the land.

Buffalo Gap National Grassland, in South Dakota, is part of North America's Great Plains.

# TEMPERATE OR TROPICAL?

Some grasslands are tropical, while others are temperate. Tropical grasslands are in the tropics, or hot regions near the equator. Temperate grasslands are found north and south of the tropics.

Tropical grasslands are often called savannas. Africa, India, Southeast Asia, South America, and Australia all have areas of savanna. The climate of savannas is extreme. Temperatures are high, and there are wet and dry seasons. During the dry season savannas get little rain.

This Kenyan savanna provides food for various animals, such as the zebras pictured here.

**COMPARE AND CONTRAST**

How are savannas and temperate grasslands alike? How are they different?

The climate in temperate grasslands is less extreme. The prairies of North America are temperate grasslands, as are the pampas of Argentina, the veld of southern Africa, the steppes of central Asia, and the huge rangelands in Australia's southeastern corner. A lot of the precipitation in temperate grasslands comes from snow rather than rain. Soil in temperate grasslands is usually rich in nutrients, which makes it good for farming.

Grain crops, such as wheat, grow well on grasslands, providing food for animals and humans alike.

# Savannas

Savannas are warm year-round, with distinct wet and dry seasons. Almost all of the rain falls during the summer. Summer is between April and September in places north of the equator and between October and March south of it.

Savannas tend to get 31 to 59 inches (80–150 centimeters) of rain each year, although some get as little as 20 inches (50 cm). The dry season is longer than the wet

The savannas of the Serengeti, in East Africa, have the heaviest rainfall between November and April.

**COMPARE AND CONTRAST**

How are a savanna's wet and dry seasons like the four seasons in temperate climates? How are they different?

season. Monthly temperatures are usually 50 to 68 degrees Fahrenheit (10-20 degrees Celsius) in the dry season and between 68°F and 86°F (20–30°C) in the wet season.

At the beginning of the rainy season streams quickly flood. In the dry seasons, the rivers return to their channels. The floodwaters leave behind rich soil after they retreat.

**Heavy rain in savannas can cause nearby rivers to overflow, flooding the plains.** ▶▶

Savanna grasses are coarse. They range from 2 to 12 feet (0.6–3.7 meters) in height. Young blades of dull green spring up rapidly at the start of the wet season. They are separated by bare spots of reddish soil. As the plants mature, the blades grow stiff and harsh. In the dry season they change to a dusty yellow or brown and slump to the ground.

Along with grasses, savannas have scattered

Termite mounds, such as this one in Botswana, are a feature of many savanna landscapes.

## THINK ABOUT IT

Why do you think savanna grasses change color and texture during the dry season? Why do you think they grow quickly during the wet season?

drought-resistant trees. Trees of the flat-topped acacia type grow at the edges of savannas in Africa and Australia. In the Llanos of Venezuela, the campos of Brazil, and the Sudan of Africa, tall grasses are mixed with low trees and thickets.

These trees with yellow flowers are prickly acacia. They are growing on a savanna in Australia.

# PRAIRIES

Prairie grasses are usually about 2 feet (0.6 m) tall, and wildflowers grow among them. The grasses also have deep roots, to allow them to get water from underground during dry periods. A striking feature of the original prairie of the United States was the vast expanse of tall grass billowing in the wind.

**Tallgrass Prairie National Preserve in Kansas is home to between forty and sixty types of grasses.**

Except for woods along streams, the natural prairie is a treeless, rolling plain.

The prairies, in general, are in regions in which the annual rainfall averages from 20 to 40 inches (50–100 cm). The heaviest amounts are in the summer.

Some prairie areas get as much rain as forests. Various explanations have been given for why grasses grow instead. The occasional dry years may have withered any young trees that were growing and allowed hardy grasses to take over. Or grass fires may have killed the **saplings**.

Indian grass (*Sorghastrum nutans*) grows easily and reseeds after wildfires clear the prairie.

# STEPPES

Steppes are found all over the world. The best-known steppe is located in Eurasia. It stretches from Hungary, in Eastern Europe, through Russia and Mongolia into northern China. North America's Great Plains—between the prairies and the Rocky Mountains—are also steppe grasslands.

Steppes experience hot summers and cold winters. They have low amounts of rainfall, from 10 to 20 inches (25–50 cm) per year.

**Steppe grasses are short because steppes don't get as much sun and water as other grasslands.**

## THINK ABOUT IT

Would a steppe be a good place for people to live? Why or why not?

Steppe grasses are short compared to wild grasses in other grasslands. They usually grow to no more than 20 inches (51 cm), and their roots are not deep. Other types of plants found there include buffalo grass and sagebrush. The soil is usually dry, so it does not make good farmland. Animals can graze there, but it is difficult to grow food.

Plants and animals struggle to thrive in the harsh environment of the steppe of Kyrgyzstan.

# THE PAMPAS

The pampas cover a large part of Argentina, a country in South America. The pampas begin at the Atlantic Coast and stretch to the foothills of the Andes Mountains. The word "pampas" comes from a **Quechua** Indian word meaning "flat surface."

The lush greenery in the pampas of the Sierra de Córdoba is a result of the heavy rains that fall.

The western pampas are dry and sandy, while the eastern pampas are humid and green. In the east, heavy rainstorms called *pamperos* sometimes occur. The

**VOCABULARY**

The Quechua are Native Americans who live in the Andes highlands from Ecuador to Bolivia.

temperature ranges from 40°F to 77°F (4–25°C).

Pampas grass is common in this biome. It does best in warm, damp soil. It can grow to be as much as 13 feet (4 m) tall. Some Pampas grass has pink flowers at its tips. Cattails, water lilies, and reeds grow in the wetter parts of the pampas.

Pampas grass seeds, found in the feathery tops, spread easily in the winds of the pampas.

# THE VELD

The veld is a grassland in southern Africa. It falls mostly within the borders of South Africa and Zimbabwe. The veld has many different levels of elevation. Because of that it is divided into three areas: the Highveld, Middleveld, and Lowveld.

The climate of the veld widely varies. Overall, however, the veld has mild winters and hot summers. The South African Highveld is typically colder than the Lowveld. Temperatures are slightly higher in Zimbabwe. Most of the rain falls

The Highveld of southern Africa is between 4,000 and 6,000 feet (1,219–1,929 m) above sea level.

in the summer months. Serious droughts occur every three or four years on the veld.

In the South African Highveld, red grass is the most common type of plant. The red grass is sweet, and animals like to graze on it. The Middleveld is drier. In some parts only thorny plants and bushes grow. In Zimbabwe, the Highveld and Middleveld are open grasslands with tall grasses and flowering herbs. The Lowveld everywhere supports a parklike plant cover. The open ground is covered by red grass. Some acacia and other trees grow there as well.

**THINK ABOUT IT**

Why do you think temperatures tend to be colder in the Highveld than the Lowveld?

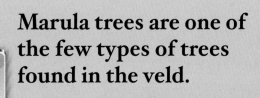

Marula trees are one of the few types of trees found in the veld.

# ANIMAL LIFE

Grasslands are home to a variety of animal species. Grasses and other plants provide a good source of food for these animals.

Animal life varies widely on the various continents. The South American savannas have capybaras, Orinoco crocodiles, jaguars, tapirs, and peccaries. Lions, leopards, zebras, giraffes, elephants, buffaloes, and other large mammals are found

Herds of antelope gather around a pool of water on the African savanna.

on the African savannas. Mosquitoes, ants, ticks, and other insects make life miserable for animals and people of the savanna. Many birds live among the trees beside the streams, especially in South America.

**COMPARE AND CONTRAST**

How is the animal life in South American and African savannas similar? How is it different?

Before settlers arrived on the prairies of North America, bison, wolves, and prairie chickens lived there. Today, only small animals are still common in the wild. Coyotes, jackrabbits, badgers, songbirds, and other animals can be found. Grasshoppers are a common insect on the prairie.

Coyotes are among the few predators that still roam freely on the open prairies of North America.

Many interesting animals live in the pampas of South America. Guanacos, which look like llamas, are found in the pampas, as are foxes, pampas deer, viscachas (a type of rodent), and rheas (large, flightless birds).

Steppes are the natural home of many animals. Large animals such as antelopes, bison, and wild sheep graze on the grasses of the steppes. However, many of those animals were killed or forced off the land as settlers moved in. Native insects, birds, reptiles, and small mammals—such as rabbits and prairie dogs—survived.

**Rheas, tall birds that live in the pampas, are in the same family of birds as ostriches and emus.**

## THINK ABOUT IT

Why do you think smaller native animals are more common after settlement than large ones are?

The activities of people also had an impact on the wildlife of the veld. Lions, leopards, cheetahs, giraffes, elephants, hippopotamus, and large antelope species survive only in protected areas, such as wildlife reserves. Smaller mammals, reptiles, and many birds are still found in the wild.

Prairie dogs burrow under the ground, popping up to the surface to find food.

25

# LAND USE

Grasslands are useful to both humans and animals. They are good places to live because they can provide food.

Animals depend on the plants that grow there for their meals. People have used grasslands in two main ways— to graze the animals they raise for food, and to grow food for themselves and their livestock.

People use some grasslands, such as steppes, mainly for grazing. They raise

Grasslands make perfect grazing grounds for sheep on the pampas in Argentina.

**COMPARE AND CONTRAST**

What are the similarities in the ways people use steppes and prairies? What are the differences?

Land that can grow wild grasses is also good for growing grain.

large groups of animals, such as sheep, goats, and cows, for the meat, milk, or wool. These animals feed on the grasses that grow on the steppe. Many more animals than people live in these grazing areas.

Prairies tend to have far more people. The soil, so rich in nutrients, is excellent for farming. People on the prairies grow food not just for themselves but also to sell to others.

# THREATS TO GRASSLANDS

Over many years people have changed much of Earth's native grassland into farmland. In North America the prairies once extended down the middle of the continent, from Canada to Texas. Now most of this land is farmland. The Australian grasslands and the South American pampas have also become mostly farming and grazing lands. Grasslands have also disappeared as cities and towns have expanded. Many of the native species

Bison nearly died out in the early twentieth century, but they have made a comeback.

have disappeared from these grasslands. When crops replaced native plants, the native animals that depended on these plants for food could not find food. Other animals died out or became rare because they were hunted so much.

Farming has even changed the soil in grasslands. Sometimes farmers plant a crop that needs more water than native plants would or that uses more nutrients from the soil. This can **deplete** the soil. Today some people are trying to protect the remaining grasslands. They teach ways of using the land responsibly to conserve the soil as well as the plants and animals that live there.

> ### VOCABULARY
>
> **To deplete something is to use it up.**

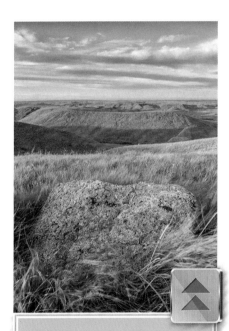

Some nations have set aside large areas of grassland as national parks.

# GLOSSARY

**climate** The weather found in a certain place over a long period of time.

**drought** A shortage of rain over a long period of time.

**flood** When water overflows onto dry land.

**elevation** The height above sea level.

**equator** An imaginary circle around Earth that divides Earth into two equal parts: the Northern Hemisphere and the Southern Hemisphere.

**graze** To feed on growing grass or herbs.

**humid** Damp, moist.

**livestock** Animals kept or raised for use and profit.

**mature** To fully grow or develop.

**native** Living or growing naturally in a place.

**nutrient** Something that living things need to grow and survive.

**plain** A broad area of level or rolling treeless country.

**precipitation** Water or the amount of water that falls to the earth as hail, mist, rain, sleet, or snow.

**species** A category of living things.

**thicket** A thick usually small patch of shrubbery, small trees, or underbrush.

**tropical** Of the tropics, a region of Earth's surface that is closest to the equator.

**temperate** A climate that is usually mild without extremely cold or extremely hot temperatures.

**wildfire** An uncontrolled fire that destroys a wide area.

# For More Information

## Books

Bjorklund, Ruth. *24 Hours in a Grassland.* New York, NY: Cavendish Square Publishing, 2018.

Callery, Sean. *Life Cycles: Grasslands.* London, UK: Kingfisher, 2018.

Gagne, Tammy. *Grassland Ecosystems* (Earth's Ecosystems). Mankato, MN: 12-Story Library, 2018.

Johansson, Philip. *The Grasslands: Discover This Wide Open Biome.* New York, NY: Enslow Elementary, 2015.

LaPlante, Walter. *There Are Grasslands in My Backyard!* New York, NY: Gareth Stevens Publishing, 2017

Spilsbury, Richard and Louise A. *Grassland Biomes.* New York, NY: Crabtree Publishing Company, 2018.

## Websites

**Easy Science for Kids**
http://easyscienceforkids.com/all-about-grasslands/
Facebook, Twitter: @EasyScienceForKids

**Kids Do Ecology: World Biomes**
http://kids.nceas.ucsb.edu/biomes/grassland.html

**National Geographic Kids**
https://kids.nationalgeographic.com/explore/nature/habitats/grassland/
Facebook: @nationalgeographickids;
Twitter: @NGKids

**San Diego Zoo**
http://animals.sandiegozoo.org/habitats/prairie-steppes
Facebook: @SanDiegoZoo; Twitter: @sandiegozoo

# INDEX